Dancing On The Edge of Normalcy

Poetry & Prose

Lydia Zorzi

the Peppertree Press
www.peppertreepublishing.com

Copyright © Lydia Zorzi, 2024

All rights reserved. Published by the Peppertree Press, LLC. The Peppertree Press and associated logos are trademarks of the Peppertree Press, LLC. No part of this publication may be reproduced, stored in a retrieval system, transmitted in any form or by any means, electronic, mechanical, photocopying, recording, or otherwise, without prior written permission of the publisher and author/illustrator. Graphic design by Elizabeth Parry.

For information regarding permission, call 941-922-2662 or contact us at our website: www.peppertreepublishing.com
or write to:
The Peppertree Press, LLC.
Attention: Publisher
715 N. Washington Blvd., Suite B
Sarasota, Florida 34236

ISBN: 978-1-61493-951-1
Library of Congress: 2024914597
Printed: September 2024

Dedication

There have been many people along my life's journey that have left a mark on me; some for the good and some for the bad.

I dedicate this book to the jewels of my life:

My husband has been with me on my journey for over 52 years. It has been a roller coaster ride.
He never lost his balance and helped anchor me.
My two children who are grown but will forever, in my heart, be my babies.
My three grandchildren who bring joy and wonder into the world.
My sister we share a bond that will never be broken.
My parents were a roadmap for my life. Though, they are no longer in the world, they are always with me.
And to friends and family who have had my back, thank you. You know who you are.

Preface

When I picked up my pen, that early February morning, I did not realize that I would be creating this work. I just felt compelled to write.

For a good part of my life, I have avoided moving towards challenges. I never looked at challenges as something to conquer. Rather, things to avoid. Now, looking at my own words, and at my life, I see that I did have to confront rather than avoid.

That morning when I first accepted the pull to answer those floating words, I could not dismiss their force. Musicians often hear a note, in their sleep, and immediately jot it down for fear that it would be lost. I think it was that sense that made me act. I, too, was afraid that my words would disappear.

I hope these words will touch a chord in you!

Most of us are dancing on an edge. It just is the human experience. The good mixes with the bad. Some days we are balanced and other days we are teetering. Many of the thoughts I share with you are mixtures of edge-dancing moments.

Unbalanced doesn't always mean negative. I can feel dizzy when I see first buds on a tree or hear a beautiful piece of music. The sheer beauty of it bringing me to tears; I am moved to depths of sadness and despair when I experience discord from those that I love.

Except for the first and last pages in this book my poems are placed randomly with no specific category. *Dancing on the Edge of Normalcy* ebbs and flows, the way that life tends to do. I hope that the reader will feel its movement.

Contents

Pen to Paper 1
Oblivion 3
Snow. 4
No Escape 5
Disappearing 6
Marginalized 8
Chip on your Shoulder 10
Crows 11
Open Wound 12
The Piece That Is Not There 13
Alone 14
Fallacy 16
Hospital Corners 17
There Is No Color 18
The End 19
"I Know...". 20
Regurgitation 21
Abuser 22
Death Bed Wish 23
A Letter to the Question 24
Agnostic Surrender 25
Righteous Indignation 26
Ripples 28
Magic Lights 29
No Solomon 30

Cutting Me Slack	31
Ants...Slugs....in the End	32
Begging for Scraps	33
Muzzle and Leash	35
A Different Mirror	36
Desert Island	37
Catalyst *(ode to Richard Chamberlain)*	38
Falling Leaves	40
Untethered	42
Cracked Vase	43
Desire	44
Broken	45
Garbage Night	46
Cacophony	47
3/4s Does Not A Whole Make	48
Baggage	49
Drought	50
Kindling	51
Festering	52
Chessboard piece	53
Street Corners	54
It's Not All…	57
A Simple Walk	58
Gone	60
Need for Pain	61
Dying Cells	62
Testosterone Den	64

Gerber Daisies 65
Ninety Minute Flight. 67
Court Jester 68
Tea Instead of Coffee 69
I Would Love.... 70
Coffee and Loss 71
Sweet Voices 72
Relegation 73
No is Not a Yes. 74
Watching you Slip 75
Starlings 76
Hands Off 78
Lighting Candles 80
Forgiveness. 81
Your Song 82
Genuflecting 83
Window Pane Lullaby 84
Lightness. 86
Am I Real 87
Heart Beat 88
Incomplete Puzzle 89

About the Author. 90

Pen to Paper

What drove me tonight...early morn
To pick up pen to paper
I tried hard to ignore the thoughts
To turn over
And reach for the bliss of nothingness
But
My mind
My soul
Kept tugging
Until I could no longer achieve
Peace or rest unless I answered
Thoughts of
Life
Death
Choices
Family
God
Raced through me
Answers sought
Questions asked
Did I think I could achieve
One bit of
Self-Discovery
Self-Elevation
Nirvana

Lydia Zorzi

What I found instead
Were pieces of a puzzle
My puzzle
Scattered

I am still unfinished

2/5/2021

Oblivion

From the moment we are born
Nay
From the moment of our conception
We begin our slide towards oblivion
Know it
Feel it
But do not let It paralyze you
Every second... every nanosecond
It is an ever present being
It rose me from my sleep tonight
Forcing me to take pen to paper
To express Its presence
See
It does not paralyze
It motivates us
To press through
To write
To think
To love
To endure
To do
This slide towards oblivion

2/5/2021

Snow

It comes as a cleansing
Bringing an opportunity
To view the world
In a moment of beauty and purity
Like a newborn soul
What can we do with it
We can pick up a shovel and clear a path
Making moving easier
We can make piles of it to climb over
An adventure
We can let the world deal with it
Ignoring our need to intervene or see
Or
We can make snow angels
Lying in it like a child with our children
Using it to make memories to be replayed
Over and over
Leaving a gift for the future

2/5/2021

No Escape

There is no escape
Oh don't despair
There will be time for beauty
Despite the ugly that may be present
Despite poor choices
Despite disappointments
Always time for beauty
For love
For memories
For deep awareness
Fill your soul
Knowing full well
We are heading to an end
Whether it be short or long
There is no escape

2/5/2021

Lydia Zorzi

Disappearing

I felt myself disappearing
Despite a comfortable life
Despite a good husband
Despite my beautiful children
Bit by bit I was becoming invisible
When I told you how I felt
You said "it's all in your head"
This feeling of inadequacy…of failure
Was a poison
I was at my 40th year mark
How could this be
So sad
No solace
Suddenly I was given a life-line
Not the best one
I did not look for it
It was tossed
I grabbed it to keep from sinking
It gave me a chance to breathe
But
Once on safe ground I realized
I had lost valuables
That I might never retrieve
I have been trying to salvage
Those jewels that I had let slip

I could not hold them
And the rope at the same time
Now I feel their loss
With every breath I take
Saving myself may have cost too much
Keeping me from disappearing
May have made them feel
That they had disappeared

2/5/2021

Marginalized

It is not in your head
It is not a fantasy
This sense that you are on the periphery
Being left behind
Being isolated
It is a reality sad to say
It is a terrible feeling
Becoming marginalized
By those who should be so close
Bit by Bit subtractions are made
Brick by Brick a fortress grows
Closing off your light
Closing off my light
Closing off OUR light
Leaving the darkness to rule
Making the way back into each other's lives
More and more difficult
Until you forget that there ever was a path
A sorry price to pay just to be safe
To avoid seeing this terrible reality
Your true history being lost

To marginalize the past
Is to marginalize the present
And worse to marginalize the future

I choose
Despite your choices
Despite the chaos
Despite the pain
Despite the battle
Despite my temptation
Not to marginalize You

7/20/21

Chip on your Shoulder

You think it is so tiny that chip
That It empowers
It keeps you vigilant
With your anger and immovability
After a while
Unknown to you
That chip is empowered
Not you
It views the world
It perceives slights
It creates an armor around you
It is an unforgiving fortress
Keeping you trapped
Imperceptibly it grows
No free thoughts from your
Mind
Soul
Heart
Only the directives
From that boulder
That has bent you
To ITS will

2/2021

Crows

My mother called me a crow
Because I liked sparkly things
Things that crows would notice

I still do
Gems
Dewdrops
Icicles
Tinsel on Christmas trees
Bright eyes of my children... grand-children
The shininess of happy smiles and laughter

There are so many moments
All around that glisten
You just need to look...to feel
Let them envelop you
You too can be a fellow crow

2/2021

Open Wound

So many chances to heal that wound
To cleanse it
Use a salve
Soothe it
Let it dry
The scab to form
Leaving it healed
Instead
You scratch it
Pouring salt to keep it festering
Looking for new ways to keep it open
Finding barbs
Real or imagined
A rolled eye
A tone not right
A glance
All for what
You achieve nothing
Except self-mutilation
Each moment lost is lost
Take the salve
Trust it will work
Let go of the pain
Close the wound
Let it be healed

6/2021

The Piece That Is Not There

RSVPs answered
Venue set
A whirl of activities abound
Glasses clinking in cheers
Tables filled with bounty
Scents and sounds fill the air
Gaiety
Camaraderie
Perfect
But
For the piece that is not there
The greater the mirth
The darker I feel
Nothing can lighten the empty space
The space where you should be
A sadness follows
Knowing that this should not be
The light that only you can hold
Now with-drawn
Casts a shadow
An emptiness at the very center of all
Leaving an incompleteness
Which fills me with despair

9/24/23

Alone

Despite
Shoulders to lean on
Prayers offered
Candles lit
Hands held
Kindnesses provided

You are alone

The pain that you feel
Cannot be felt by others
Can anyone truly appreciate
The depth of
Fear
Anguish
Isolation
That encases you
Your self-control
Your smiles
Forced as they may be
Prevents the release of this pain
Shout Out
Give Vent

Now is not the time
To worry about their comfort

They will move on

They have time

7/28/2021

Lydia Zorzi

Fallacy

Thinking that I make a difference
Believing that my thoughts matter
Saying that I am artistically different
Rather
Than just a nuisance
Not wanting to be in that
Bell Curve of Mediocracy
Being an outlier
A preferred position
Flights of frank speech
Monologues for myself
Actions
Perceived as socially conflicted
Deeming them all to be freeing
Fallacy
Self-delusional
I will leave no lasting thread
Sadly
No tapestry of beauty or worth
Will be woven by me

11/25/23

Hospital Corners

You taught us
How to make a perfect hospital bed
The sheets so smooth
No wrinkles to be seen
Corners tucked precisely
It had to be just so for grading

You warned us
That it would never be as perfect
Outside our class

In the real world
There would be too many pressures
Time would have to be measured
But
"If we learned it correctly"
We would never stray so far
As to make it wrong
Who knew that making a bed
And your words
Would carry so much weight in my Life

4/21/24

Lydia Zorzi

There Is No Color

A mother kisses her child
Tickles his toes
Strokes her hair
Cradles them gently
Smiling in wonderment to herself
Love shines on her face
On the faces
Of all those who love
It has no Color in mind
Its look does not differ
Shinning the same
On the faces of those who offer it
And to those who receive it

9/23/2021

The End

If the End were to come
The world ceasing to exist
Who would you choose to be with
In that final goodbye
Friends
Lovers
Family
Alone
Have you ever taken the time
To sit with this thought

I have

Despite the craziness that often surrounds
The answer is always the same

It is you

It always has been

It always will be

10/2021

Lydia Zorzi

"I Know..."

When I speak with you
About things that concern
Detailing the wrongs...issues
That need to be addressed
You say
"I know...I know..."
Knowing is the first step
An awareness
It is not the same as changing
To see you continue on the same track
Taking you to the same platform
A place you don't want to be
Is hurtful
There are times
I wish I could walk away
Leaving you
Stranded
Alone
On that desolate platform
Pretending that all is well
That would be too hard to bear
For you...For me

11/1/2021

Regurgitation

Yell
Spit it out
Let's deal with it
The hurts
The accusations
I won't like the ugliness
Still
It may be cathartic
I will accept the pain
If it cleanses the space
But
Don't bring it back up
Once that door is closed
Let it stay shut
So
When I turn to enter
I will not need to fear
A wall of stale
Regurgitated
Recriminations

11/2/2021

Abuser

Narrow foyer
Dark and musty
Cigarette scented
A flickering TV screen
Traffic sounds from an open window
Naked women on a calendar
Smudged image of a face
A trusted neighbor
Two little girls…sisters
A mother's prayers
Cries of despair
Recollected by the younger of the two
Images blurred
No sense of pain
Dulled perhaps to escape

The child moves through the years
Even praying
On occasion
For her
Abuser

Death Bed Wish

Years ago
When my family was young
And so was I
A question was asked
That if I were at life's end
What would have made it all worthwhile

So many choices
Power
Riches
Fame

For me
Simply
That my family would be
Loving
Caring
Fulfilled
Tied to one another

How sad to know
That if I were on that bed now

My life's wishes would be unfinished

2/2021

A Letter to the Question

I think of the possibility of a You
Occasionally
In tiny snippets
Some days more than others
I try to understand
To feel You
No truths are revealed
Your feasibility is in question
Your importance is too
Does it really matter
If I solve Your riddle
I could simply choose not to question
To make You disappear
To go through life with one less mystery
To burden me
Somehow
That doesn't feel right
Or is it that I am afraid to let go
Does Your possibility keep me feeling safer
Or do I think
That I might be a lesser person
Without the possibility of a You

1/8/2022

Agnostic Surrender

It is exhausting sitting on the fence
Turning over the same stone
Looking for a new perspective
Questions asked...answers sought
When one is offered...reevaluating it
Questioning
I am told
Is a sign of intelligence
Of a mind not placed on pause
It gave me great pleasure to hear
Was it hubris
No answer have I
Except that even the most beautiful gift
If overly scrutinized
Can be found to have a fault
The same can be said for sitting on a fence
Pleased with being able to observe both sides
Safe
Neither here nor there
With your feet never committed
I can't ...I won't do it anymore
I have chosen to land on a side
Your side
Wrong or Right
I can no longer remain in neutral territory

3/20/2022

Righteous Indignation

"The world is ugly"
Today I uttered words
That have never escaped my mouth
I feel the drag of them
Pulling me into darkness
An abyss

Where are the rainbows
That I could always conjure up
Despite the chaos of my life
I don't see them today

At this moment
They are not only obliterated
By the darkness
They have ceased to exist
The ugly has swallowed my soul
Buried it in
Guilt
Helplessness
Hurt
Fear

Believe me

I understand your pain

It is the deliberate choice
To bury yourselves
Under righteous indignation
Taking me along
That I cannot grasp
Today
The world is an ugly place

7/9/2022

Lydia Zorzi

Ripples

The stillness of the quiet waters
Can be stirred into life
By the simplest of movements
A gentle breeze
An alighting of a dragonfly
Swirling ripples appear
Moving across the quietude
Until thy gently ebb
And the stillness returns

So too can our hearts
Be nudged into wakefulness
A scent
A sound
A touch
We find ourselves
Crying
Smiling
Remembering
Lost in a reverie
Our Hearts...Minds...Souls
Have recognized a past mark left upon them
And a ripple stirs

3/2022

Magic Lights

Summer is here
And with it comes
Glittering bits of lights
Twinkling on and off
Magical
Staying for just a short time
They can be held in your hand
Or in a jar
Released back into the night
But
If you let yourself
Be caught up in their glow
That light will keep
In your heart
Well after they are gone

9/5/22

No Solomon

Unlike Solomon
I have no ability to save the "baby"
Either choice I make
Would result in the perception
That a child had to be sacrificed
Two children
One mother
Pulled in opposite directions
Staying neutral
Makes him feel that he is on the altar
Pleading to her to offer an olive branch
Gives her the sense of being sacrificed
So
They have placed that beautiful "baby"
Their blood ties on the altar
Of
Pride
Righteous Indignation
Hurt
Where it awaits to die
And I alas
Am no Solomon

7/2022

Cutting Me Slack

You think that you are being so kind
When you offer me some "slack"
As if I had some embarrassing short comings
That you have to make light
The things that you see as being
On the cusp of Normalcy
Are the very things I like best
What you call strange
I call different
I call it being ME

10/27/22 edit

Lydia Zorzi

Ants...Slugs....in the End

Ants
Working unceasingly
Slugs
Barely moving
It may seem that diligence would bring
The greater reward
For a short temporary time
It may well be so
People running like ants
People moving like slugs

The ending is the same for all

Perhaps the ones who meander slowly
Are actually harvesting better along the way
Than the ones who slave away
Gathering and hoarding
That which will not have much
Worth or merit
At the conclusion of it all

5/23 2/24

Begging for Scraps

Like a hungry dog
I sit with hopefulness
That a piece of your bounty
Will feed me
It is such a lonely place to be
Begging for morsels of affection
Of forgiveness
Knowing that I may have placed
Myself in this position
Only accentuates the pain

I hunger for a pat on the head
For some kind acceptance
For just a morsel
Here I wait
Alone
With dying hope

A devastating realization dawned
The table of bounty
From where a morsel might fall
Was not manned by you
But

Lydia Zorzi

By me
You waiting for a morsel

It was a heartbreaking vision
That I who should be a good
Could be so hurtful
To you who are the centers of my heart

Let the embers of hope glow
That the table will become one of bounty
Not of scraps
Leaving
Neither one alone
Neither one hungry

5/11/2023

Muzzle and Leash

Why do I feel that
You would love
To keep me silent
Never letting me explore too far
Or too much
Like a dog on a leash
With its mouth muzzled
The poor thing allowed only
What you want it to do
For its sake...its benefit
Or
To protect yourself
From the fallout that might occur
If it chose to wander
Giving voice to its demands
I may have allowed you
To place those items on me
In my younger complacent days
But
I will bite
Howling loudly
If it is ever tried again

9/7/2022

Lydia Zorzi

A Different Mirror

I saw through a different mirror
An ugly something
Caged
Curled up
Ready to spring
Trying to escape the padlocked cage
The heavy blanket thrown over it
Could not keep its poison from leaching out
Malevolent...damaging
I saw clearly
Not wanting to believe
The scars that it had left
On those who had come too close
To Me

9/8/2022

Desert Island

I feel a calming respite
When I am with myself
Alone
With just me
In my own company
It is not isolating
Thoughts wonder through my mind
Plans for now and the future are created
No one other than myself
Can critique me
I am free to be me
To explore
At my leisure
At my pace
My ideas can be shared
If I choose
Without concern of offending
Or embarrassing
Those who are most valuable to me
I can be my own Desert Island
Where there are no eggshells to worry about
And being with myself is effortless

3/2023

Catalyst
(ode to Richard Chamberlain)

It's been years since we spent time together
I remember those moments
As if it were yesterday
Your smile so blindingly bright
Almost as white as your uniform
Down to your shoes
Dramatically
You would rush through the halls
Bringing salvation to those in need
Oh
How I looked forward to our evenings
Limited in time as they were
Blue eyes so serene
Blond hair always in place
I could almost smell your soap scented aura
You were unlike any man I knew
You moved through chaos in a calmness
Unknown to me
Your presence
Even for that short hour
Brought lightness into my darkness
How I suffered through failures
Cheered at your successes
Raged with jealousy at interlopers
You were my first crush

But time passed
I grew up
Wore a uniform of white
Walked similar halls
You became a pleasant memory
But no longer a player in my life
Then
Fortunately or Not
Life brought us back together
This time you wore robes of black
You entered my life at a delicate point
My 40th year
Enmeshed
Watching your choices
Made me question mine
Your failed happy ending
Capsized me
I would make better choices
I would not fail
Or so I thought

My dear

You were quite the Catalyst

2021

Falling Leaves

Autumn leaves
With varied shapes and sizes
Depending on their origin
Colors brilliant
Golds
Reds
Bronzes
All clinging to life
None wanting to fall...any earlier than need
The elements of the world
Imposing dictates
Despite the urge to remain
Some hardier than others
Others luckier
But in the end
They will all loosen their hold
And fall
Creating a multicolored carpet underfoot
For all to appreciate

Humanity echoes
Colors
Shapes
Powers of the world
Clinging

Struggling
Falling
Our essences
Our individual threads
Woven into a multicolored tapestry
Flung into the world
Hopefully to be embraced

11/2023

Lydia Zorzi

Untethered

A small little old woman
A small little old dog
She in her house dress and slippers
Her companion untethered by a leash
Walking slowly together
Side by side
The sweetness of the moment struck me
Two old friends leisurely enjoying the time
No rush
No cares
Both trusting that neither would stray
No physical binding keeping them tied
But
Certainly
An invisible cord of camaraderie was present
A fearful though
Flittered through my happy reverie
It would only take
A small mis-step
A distraction
To render the bond broken
They
We
Forever separated

7/2021

Cracked Vase

We were speaking of Jesus
How he presented Himself
After His death
Not in a perfect unblemished form
Rather
With His wounds manifest to be seen
His body was like a cracked vase
Intact but with imperfections
Only through those hurts
Could we understand
The gift He had given to us

Perfection
Keeping human frailties out of the equation
Unattainable

We with our
Cracks
Hurts
Imperfections
Bleeding out into the world
Vulnerable but still intact
See our light
Use it
We are of good

5/8/2023

Desire

I was nonchalantly looking about
Not searching
I caught a glimpse of you
Among hundreds of others
In that small space
My curiosity was piqued
Drawn to you like a bee to sweet nectar
Exotic coloration made you powerful
Your softness made you comforting
You had me enticed
I envisioned myself
Wrapped in your glory
I wanted you desperately
But I knew you would make me pay dearly
Only in my dreams could I enjoy you
You and I did not belong
Resisting temptation I turned my back
I walked away
I left you there
Certain that someone braver than I
Would embrace you
Taking you home
To be worn at some gala
That I could never attend

2/10/24

Broken

Like a dam eroded by wear
Lightning striking a weakened tree
Hail hurtling at a fragile window pane
In a simple unexpected moment
I broke
All it took was a disheveled bed
And your unawareness of it all
I heard something give way in my head
Was this how a seizure would feel
The abyss between where I was
And where you were was unfathomable
Fists clenched
Words trying to escape
A desire to leap over
Grab those braids
To shake you into really seeing
Paralyzed by the absurdity of the moment
Just a disheveled bed
With a loved one lying in a random heap
Despite
All those degrees and licenses
How could you be trusted
If you could not see
The greater meaning of it all

10/27/22

Lydia Zorzi

Garbage Night

Hurrying through the day
Endless tasks to complete
Mundane but necessary
Tracking my "to do" list
Crossing off completed items
Adding new ones for tomorrow
Before retiring to bed
One last task…garbage night
Exiting out the door
Thinking of the task at hand
When by chance
I glanced upwards
Stopping in awe
Of the beauty that silently
Watched down over me
The large glowing moon
Brightly lite the night's dark velvety sky
A halo of mist creating
A haunting sense of mystery
And I
With garbage bag in hand
Was moved to tears
By the sudden
Unexpected
Beauty of it all

9/27/23

Cacophony

The sound surrounded me
Coming from all directions
Standing in the darkness it was glorified
Glints of light beckoning
Untouchable in the far sky
Quiet shadows
Giving coverage to the hidden life
The intensity of the moment
Magically calming

Unlike the sound that echoes
Often
Through my mind
Disquieting
Painfully off key
My spirit shudders
A cacophony of sound
That only I can hear

9/3/2022

3/4s Does Not A Whole Make

Things in life are often measured in 3/4s
Time   8:45
Baking   3/4cup
Music   3/4tempo
Life can be measured as such
75 years   3/4 of a century
3/4's of life spent in fulfilling
Duties
Responsibilities
Obligations
Not always as dreary as it may sound
Essential
Otherwise
The world would not revolve
However
It came to me
That there must be
A loose 1/4 floating around
Find it…Grab it…Create a whole
Finding it is not only desirable
It is necessary
Elsewise
We may never be more than a ¾ person

4/22/2023

Baggage

We've all heard about baggage
No
Not the kind that carries clothing
Rather the carrying of memories
Good or bad
Things that have happened to us
Things that were done by us
Occasionally we admit
That it is our baggage that is at fault
Most often
We believe everyone else's is bigger
Than ours
Until we try to place it into a compartment
As if we were placing our suitcase
Into an overhead
And find that it is so large
The size of a trunk
Not a backpack
That
No matter how hard we try to push our load
Or manipulate it
It just can't squeeze into that tight bin
And then all our carefully packed "stuff"
Spills out into the world

5/13/2023

Drought

A dry well
Day in and day out
Buckets drawn
In hopes
That some residual is found
No rain in sight to replenish it

Don't be a parasite
Make sure that you take care
Give
Give
Contort yourself into a pretzel
Make sure that needs are met
Keep doing it
Despite it being given only one way

No replenishment in sight

I have become a dry well

9/10/2022

Kindling

Waiting
Alone
Even when surrounded by a crowd
Empty eyed
Soul
Spirit
Shucked out
Denuded of essence
Reduced to kindling
For self-serving fires
Takers
Plunderers
Absorbing their glow
Leaving the givers
Enveloped in darkness
Their spark burnt away
Only the pain of loss
Reminding them
That once
They
Had value

8/2/2022

Festering

Like a cancer
Rancor is seeded
Silently making itself at home
Festering
Sending out its malevolent tentacles
Invading the healthy parts of us
At first
A war is fought by that which is good
But soon
The invasion overwhelms

Like the insidiousness of cancer
A single mutated cell escapes
Undetected
Alone
It starts to take the healthy
Transforming them into its allies
The sickness triumphs
Capitulation
The festering hate
Explodes
Obliterating the Soul

10/06/23

Chessboard piece

You had to explain to me
Optics...Networking
Not that I didn't know the definitions
Often associated
With corporate ladder climbing
But in the context of our talk
It was not understood
When you explained I was taken aback
Children in daycare
Innocent and trusting
And you all concerned about
Their appearances and connections
How they present
With whom they interact
Instead of their just being
What a load...
Placed on their small shoulders
Like chessboard pieces
Positioning themselves
Strategies that must be learned
To ensure they are not captured
Sadly disconcerting
But perhaps I am simply
An antique

9/1/2022

Lydia Zorzi

Street Corners

Ladies and men of the night
And sometimes of the day
Loitering on their preferred corners
Displaying their wares
Dressed to get noticed
To be chosen
For their paid services
These I was aware of
Their presence known since I was a child
Seen on television for entertainment
Read about in papers after a sweep
But
You showed me ones
That I did not know existed
Men gathered in groups
Or singularly
Who with a cup of coffee
Forged their way to spots
To be seen on corners
Hoping that someone would buy
Their services
Not deterred by the weather
The scorching summer sun
Wilting even the hardiest ones
The freezing winter's winds turning

Men into bent angles
Hoping to deflect its biting anger
They refused to surrender
Praying for a car to pull up
To invite them in
For at least that day a job
What was said
What was offered
I was not privy to know
But the relief of the men
Lucky enough to be chosen
As a body for cheap labor
I could discern
A pang of sorrow and pain
Rippled through me
Understanding their plight
Undocumented
Afraid
But willing to risk it all
To feed their families
Knowing that you my friend
With your own struggles
Could have become
One of those corner laborers
Brought it home to me

Lydia Zorzi

Now
Whenever I see such gatherings
That sense of
Anger
Unease
Sympathy
Sadness
Arises anew
My eyes are not blinded
To those Street Corners
And to those who rely on them

7/29/2021

It's Not All...

"It is not all about you"
You eagerly point out to me
But
When is it about me

Ever

Certainly
Not from you
I ask for recognition
Showing my need
Only to be ignored
Is it any wonder
That sometimes
I must make it
About ME

3/2024

Lydia Zorzi

A Simple Walk

Just an outing to get some steps
Nothing particular in mind
I felt my shoes sink into the warm sand
The soft particles leaching into my soles
Softly without effort

It awakened an awareness

Peaceful sounds and sights surrounded me
Waves gently lapped the edge of the shore
Children's laughter chimed
Like magical bells
Lovers
Families
Singles
Awaiting the anticipated sunset
With expectations of joy
I was engulfed by a wave of gratitude

Immediately
A second wave of emotion
Caught me unguarded
Elsewhere in the world
People were scanning the skies
Trembling with fear

Bare feet trotted on broken ground
Children's voices silenced

Peace and harmony absent

My heart ached
Envisioning the rapture
That could be realized
If my space would be theirs too

2/29/2022

Gone

You are gone
Not dead
Just gone

By your own hand
You banished yourself

That action
Banished us too
Making us gone
Not dead

Your reasons may be true
The need vital for you

Leaving us to grieve
The loss of one so loved
The loss of our WE

Not dead
But none the less
Gone

2/28/24

Need for Pain

I believe that at the very moment
There is a you...a person...a life
All of your being is set
A soul
Despite my questions about God
I cannot see your little being not having one

Those who deny your humanity astound me
They have blinded themselves
How else could they deny you
Even if you take a higher power
Out of the equation
How can 2+2=5
A small one-celled ameba is alive
It retreats when pain is inflicted
And yet they deny yours
We plead for Rights...Equality...Justice
While denying yours

Sometimes I think
We are too competent in our forgetfulness
Pain reminds the body of an illness
We should feel our moral pain
So that we can truly realize
How sick we have become

2/21/2021

Dying Cells

Waiting for sleep
Listening to the breathing next to me
I could not help but feel
The dying of my cells
With each passing second
Pieces of me were being lost
Time does not stop or slow
Moving ever forward
Trampling all
On its blind roll
Knowing that this is the cycle for all beings
Does not lessen the melancholy of loss
Rather
It makes you think
Should've
Could've
Would've
Knowing that some of my choices
Have left my cells in turmoil
I wonder if they will
Simply
Suddenly
Cease to exist
Or will they fight to the very end
Lingering like embers

Grasping for more time
To remember
To be remembered
After they are gone
After I am gone

Tonight I am afraid

3/24/23

Lydia Zorzi

Testosterone Den

I did not know what to expect
Entering a shop such as yours
Small and dark
Minimal decorative touches
Men sitting about
Lazily interacting
The air ladened with thick smoke
The room impregnated
With the aroma of cigars
The scent of testosterone was surprising
Calming
My presence raised a curious look
Assuring them that I was not a spy
They laughed
Acceptance without a struggle
A community was present...a refuge
Sipping on scotch
Talking about fine flavors of life
A presentation of a homemade meal
Eaten on laps
I left feeling exhilarated
Surprised at a lovely few hours
Spent in a Testosterone Den

9/2/2022

Gerber Daisies

We passed a tiny strip of green
Fenced in
To protect it from the outside
A frail little old woman
Bent and gnarled
Was tending it with loving care
I was pulled by my heart
To stop and admire
While your little hand in mine
Pulled at me to continue along
Gerber Daisies
Two or three
Reached upwards with their colorful halos
Despite
There being not much else
In that tiny patch of soil
They seemed to fill the place
For a moment
That gardener
A little old woman
And I
A young mother
Shared a connection
She tending to her garden
And I to my son
The tugging of your little hand

Lydia Zorzi

Moved us along
You did not realize
My boy
That stopping had cost nothing
But
It had given something
To this very day Gerber Daisies
And that memory of you and I
Remains special
Simply
Because of that brief stop
Along our way

8/21/2021

Ninety Minute Flight

Their prime has passed
The legs and bodies
No longer rugged or strong
Yet
As they don their cleats onto
The field of uneven terrain
I can glimpse the vigor of their past youth
In the heart of the player
Lives "La Passión"
Their flight across the field
Fighting for the goal is magnificent
Aged warriors
A testament to life
The legs may not be graceful
Missed moments occur
But
Is this play no less beautiful
Than
When the athlete in his prime
Juggles the ball
Despite the ravages of time
The Soul
For those ninety minutes
Flies

6/22/2022

Court Jester

Your self-deprecating humor
An armor against a world
That taunted you
For
Not fitting its acceptable
Body Image
Despite your intelligence and kindness
That was what was seen
Years of deflecting insults
By insulting yourself
Has followed you from childhood on
I cringe each time I hear you
Denigrating the you
That I know is so much more
You don't need to be a court jester anymore

9/8/2022

Tea Instead of Coffee

I know that there are truths
Most of my truths
Whether being taught
Or found through observation
Have been absorbed to my very core
Kindness
Justice
"Doing unto others"
Does not mean I always follow
Still I know that they are real

Choices are made
Rationalization is used
For the ones made poorly

If I give you tea instead of coffee
Mistake
Stepping on a Truth
Choice
I hate how it feels when I stand exposed
Accepting my poor choices
What I hate even more
Is when you say that what you did
Was simply give me Tea instead of Coffee

3/20/2021

Lydia Zorzi

I Would Love...

I would love to believe in the Baby Jesus born onto us. Who grew into manhood and then died for all.
Children have this gift of belief. I see it when they pass the Nativity scene. Their eyes and voices light at the sight of the Baby lying in the manger. To them, He is as real as Santa Claus!
I, too, remember being in awe at the scene. Feeling a sadness for Him so tiny and helpless. Lying wrapped in a cloth. Poor in a dark stable. A gift for us!
Kneeling at the Church rail, looking up at the crucified Christ, I would think of the Child that He had once been. Tears cascading, thinking of the cruelty of men. He hung on the cross as a man but in my heart, I saw the innocent Christmas Baby.
When does the magic in children's eyes, minds and hearts disappear? It's there one moment and then like a mist away it floats. Oh, how I would love to be able to retrieve it again. To feel the awe and the pain that Jesus should elicit in my heart. Our hearts. To believe, simply, like a child once again!

12/24/23

Coffee and Loss

A routine day
Coffee in the kitchen
Before heading off to work
Weekend plans in my head
Not a mother yet
But
Carrying my firstborn
A snippet of news
Iced me with shock
Little...Innocent...Alone
To catch that school bus that morn
Before your weekend plans
Like a big boy
How brave you must have felt
You rounded the corner
And
Disappeared
In that moment
Life and lives were forever changed
Mine included
The sense of a world
Where children could be safe
Vanished along with you

11/21/23

Sweet Voices

While at mass today
Lost in a state of distraction
Listening to adult voices
Speaking the words that should
Guide... Inspire... Elevate
Songs being song by the congregation
All falling on my almost deaf ears
Suddenly
I was I brought into a realm of beauty

Innocent and sweet
Children's voices had replaced
The utterances of the adults
Bringing me to tears
It was closer to prayerfulness
Than any part of the service
It touched my heart
Knowing that at that moment
They were closer to God
Than any adult present
Beautiful... Bittersweet
Soon
They would enter into the world
Their sweetness jeopardized
So
I listened with my heart
While their grace blessed me

5/22/2023

Relegation

Thinking that you can place
Some events in a closet
Keeping them in the dark
As if they never happened
Your very life
As it is now
As it will move into the future
Is intimately connected
To indelible moments
Your mother giving birth to you
Your lover giving life to your son
I with your life journey
Friendship no longer suffices
You want what was once
The hurt comes not from change
But being viewed from a rearview mirror
Forgetting
That the who you are
The who you will be
Is directly related to moments
The past
The present
The future
Rolling through your very bones

10/27/22

Lydia Zorzi

No is Not a Yes

You say that you love me
You say that I am yours
That our history is so strong
Yes it is strong
But it should not control
You refuse to hear me
I tell you
That it is not good for me
It takes my peace
It damages the person I want to be
You don't or won't believe it
You feel hurt
Seeing you hurt
Makes me weak
Because
I am used to healing you
I ask you to hear
I plead for you to understand
You refuse
I hate manipulators
I hate weak women
You know this to be true
But you turn me into one
When you take a No for a Yes

7/18/2021

Watching you Slip

My heart aches watching you slip
Slowly away
A fading of the man I have known
For half of my life
The light in your eyes
The portals to your soul
Has dimmed
I reach out
Your response is slow
Your thoughts are tumbled
I know that you are still here
But layers of cloudiness
Makes it hard to find you
And
For you to find us
I think of wasted moments
Of memories
That could have been sown
Squandered
Hoping that there will be enough
Moments left
To soften what is to come

9/11/2022

Lydia Zorzi

Starlings

A glimpse of hope
Eyes widened
With expectation
An alertness appeared
The first seen
In weeks

You laid propped up
On your sick bed
A bed you had not left for weeks
In a room that had adopted you

Facing a window

Your eyes to see nature
If desired...though none existed
Till
A flock of blackness
Descended into the yard
Wings fluttering
Starlings creating a carpet
Layer upon layer of them
Obliterating the ground
That early minted day

A sign from God
You thought
You prayed
A blessed message
You would be lifted Heavenwards
On black wings
Relieving you of the pain
That encased you
Freedom to be yours again
Joy was what you felt
Despair was what you were left with
As those birds rose skyward

Leaving you behind

12/2023

Hands Off

I have been searching for answers
That would give me
Some sense of understanding
Thinking about the different concepts
Of who God is

As a child He was seen as an all knowing
All involved Being
Nothing happened in the world
Without His say so
We mere humans could not comprehend
This may be true or not
But
Long ago I decided
That I had my own picture of God

If He exists

He is a hands off Deity
Nothing else makes sense
Because
Who could honor a God
Who could churn out such ugliness
Simply because He can
He takes free will seriously

We live into a mortal world
A mortal world where
Hate
Disease
Exists

Seeing it as such
Allows me to continue
To believe in His possibility
Any other view would make me run
From a Father
Who could be so arbitrarily cruel
In His love

10/10/23

Lydia Zorzi

Lighting Candles

It is still a wonder
That people light candles
Praying for their wishes
To be granted
Akin
To rubbing a Genie's Lamp
Or wishing upon a star
How many of these glowing tributes
I wonder
Have resulted in an answer

Who am I to judge
Just because I have not seen
Does not mean it has not happened
What I do know
Is that it gives solace to the petitioners
To those who despair
Perhaps
That alone makes it miraculous

1/2/2022

Forgiveness

Let go of the past
Forgive yourself
I am told
How wonderful that would be
A clean slate
It shouldn't be so hard
Especially when so desired

If it wasn't for the fallout
That I face
Daily
From transgressions of the past

Sadly

I am allowed no self-absolution

5/23

Your Song

Sing your Song my Son
Sing your Song my Daughter
Sing a song of the Past
Remembering the lyrics
Containing
Beauty
Family
Love
The Present one you sing
Has forgotten those Moments
Push past the haze
Let them weave into your now
A song filled with
Isolation
Anger
Hurt
It is not the whole of you
Make it True
Make it Complete
Make it Your Song

11/12/23

Genuflecting

Often have I knelt
For the sake of Peace
Beseeching Forgiveness
Knowing full well
That the sin
Was not mine

01/2024

Lydia Zorzi

Window Pane Lullaby

Tap...Tap ...Tap
A warm sunny summer day
Alone
On my bed
The blinds drawn
On that one solitary window
Bright outside
From the summer sun
Dark inside
Protected from the rays
A book by my side
Sleepily listening
No angry voices
From my parents
No sense of chaos present
Alone
Adrift
In a welcomed
Rare
Unexpected Peace
In that three-room apartment
That was my childhood home
Tap... Tap...Tap...
A warm breeze
Creates movement from the blinds

A peaceful solitary sound
Reassuring
I welcomed its gentleness

I have lived 70 years plus
Years
Filled with treasured moments
But
The sound of a blind
Tapping
Against a windowpane
Can send me back
Transported
To that rare quiet day
And I, again, experience
The utter peace
Of a windowpane lullaby

7/2021

Lydia Zorzi

Lightness

Hellos over
Launching into a monologue
Thoughts...images
Twisting onto each other
Like Lava from an erupting volcano
A torrid of words
Came spewing at you
Not sure
If you were buried
Beneath the debris
Lost
Worse
Thinking that you were somewhere else
Not present
A nod
A hand gesture
A simple question
Showed
You were with me
Time over
Exiting out into the world
My spirit felt lightened
Had I emptied pieces of myself
Or
Had you filled me with your essence

2022

Am I Real

Sometimes I think
I am a figment
Of my imagination
A self-creation
A wisp of air
With no substance
Pretending to be me
A projection of what I think
The world expects
Certainly
I know how to reflect
Outwards
Behaviors
Responding to triggers
Like a programed robot
Allowing me to exist
But not really be
Am I really Real

12/12/23

Lydia Zorzi

Heart Beat

My sister texted saying
She heard the sun's heartbeat today
I marveled at the beauty
Of that thought
"The sun's heartbeat…"
I whispered the words to myself
How poetic
How blessed was that moment for her
A video of this miraculous moment
Was attached
I listened to hear
But
No magical sound was discerned
Disappointed
I strained my eyes
Staring at that glowing life-giving orb
Imperceptibly
Softly
Slowly
Making itself known
From deep inside
Earth's special star
The pulsation
Of the sun's heart
Appeared

3/2024

Incomplete Puzzle

There are pieces
Of the puzzle
Missing
It is not whole
The temptation is to discard
Please don't
Can't you see
What it might look like
Despite the empty spaces
It could be quite beautiful
Believe
The pieces are not lost
Simply
Misplaced…Scattered
And can be found
If
We try hard enough
IT
WE
Can be completed
Made whole
So please
Do not discard

6/2023

About the Author

Lydia is a first generation American. She grew up in Brooklyn in the 1950's living in a three-room apartment in a fifth-floor walk-up. As a child, she was shy and found respite in reading books. They offered an escape from the chaotic life that surrounded her. The years and life moved on. She became a nurse, wife, mother and grandmother. At the age of 70 she wrote her first poem and from that, this book. Life continues to ebb and flow. Chaos intermingles with harmony. Chances to change and grow are ever present. Whether there will be other writings, from Lydia, is unknown. But, for now, she is pleased that this dream has been realized!